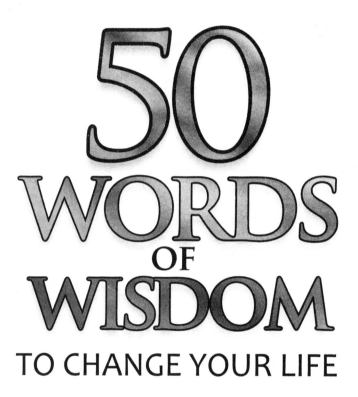

50 WORDS OF WISDOM

TO CHANGE YOUR LIFE

Dr. D. K. Olukoya

50 WORDS OF WISDOM TO CHANGE YOUR LIFE

© 2015 EDITION

Dr. D. K. Olukoya

ISBN 978-978-920-122-8

A publication of
MOUNTAIN OF FIRE AND MIRACLES MINISTRIES
13, Olasimbo Street, Off Olumo Road,
(by Unilag 2nd Gate, Onike, Iwaya)
P. O. Box 2990, Sabo, Yaba Lagos, Nigeria.
☎ 08095423392, 08095419853

Email: mountainoffireandmiraclespress@yahoo.com
Website: www.mfmbooks.co.za

All scriptures are quoted from the
King James Version of the Bible.

I salute my wonderful wife, Pastor Shade, for her
invaluable support in the ministry. I appreciate her
unquantifiable support in the book ministry as the cover
designer, art editor and art adviser.

CONTENTS

IT IS POSSIBLE TO ENTERTAIN DEMONS AS WELL AS ANGELS UNAWARES!

IF YOU DO NOT FIGHT, YOU CANNOT CONQUER. *69*

FLIES DO NOT PERCH UNTO A HOT POT: IF YOU ARE ON FIRE, CERTAIN THINGS CANNOT HAPPEN TO YOU. *72*

IF YOU MAKE YOURSELF A MOUSE, THE CAT WILL CATCH YOU. *75*

IF YOU STAND NEUTRAL, THEN YOU STAND FOR NOTHING. *78*

THE NATIONAL ANTHEM OF HELL FIRE IS: "EVERYONE IS DOING IT." *81*

FORCE YOURSELF TO PRAY BEFORE YOU ARE FORCED TO PRAY. *84*

IT IS NOT HARD TO TELL A LIE, BUT IT IS HARD TO TELL ONLY ONE LIE. *87*

NO ONE CAN LOOK DOWN ON YOU WHEN YOU ARE TALLER THAN THEY ARE. *90*

Dr. D. K. Olukoya

THE SHEPHERD THAT SLEEPS NEVER SEES HEAVENLY VISITATION.

WE CANNOT GET ANCIENT RESULTS UNTIL WE REVISIT ANCIENT PRACTICES.

IT WAS THE PRIMITIVENESS OF PETER, JAMES AND JOHN THAT GAVE THEM THRONES IN HEAVEN.

IT IS WHAT YOU KNOW THAT WILL MAKE YOU KNOWN.

IT TAKES GIANTS TO GIVE BIRTH TO GIANTS.

IT TAKES A BIRD TO HAVE FEATHERS.

A TREE THAT IS NOT TALLER THAN YOU CANNOT SHADE YOU.

LOVE GOD AND YOU WILL LOVE GOD'S PEOPLE WHEREVER YOU GO.

PERFECT PEACE COMES TO OUR HEARTS THROUGH OBEDIENCE.

ALLOW CRITICISM TO SHAPE, BUT NOT CONTROL YOU.

Introduction

Psalms 78:1-4

Give ear, O my people, to my law: incline your ears to the words of my mouth. I will open my mouth in a parable: I will utter dark sayings of old: Which we have heard and known, and our fathers have told us. We will not hide them from their children, shewing to the generation to come the praises of the LORD, and his strength, and his wonderful works that he hath done.

The quality of your life is determined by the type of books you read and by the type of words you listen to and meditate upon. Words can radically change and transform your life. There are inspirational sayings that can be used by God to give you the opportunity to reinvent your life and fulfil your destiny. No matter the present state of your life, no matter the level of problem you are battling with at the moment, there are deep words that can grant you a new orientation and subsequently mould your life and make you the type of person God wants you to be.

THE POWER OF WORDS

Words can encourage or discourage you. Words can pull down or build up. Words can introduce far-reaching changes into your life. Words can set you on fire and revolutionalise your life. This book is a collection of deep sayings that have been preserved for this generation. During the ministry of the Lord Jesus Christ, He made use of parables and deep sayings. These parables constituted a powerful vehicle for conveying to His disciples and followers, words of eternal value.

Matthew 13:10-13:
And the disciples came, and said unto him, Why speakest thou unto them in parables? He answered and said unto them, Because it is given unto you to know the mysteries of the kingdom of heaven, but to them it is not given. For whosoever hath, to him shall be given, and he shall have more abundance: but whosoever hath not, from him shall be taken away even that he hath. Therefore speak I to them in parables: because they seeing see not; and hearing they hear not, neither do they understand.

WORDS OF WISDOM

In the Old Testament, parables and wise saying were used as vehicles for conveying weighty things that have the capacity to transform and radically change lives. It is, therefore, a great privilege when powerful sayings, referred to as words of wisdom are written in black and white for the purpose of inspiration, instruction, prophetic guidance and correction.

1 Timothy 4:15
Meditate upon these things; give thyself wholly to them; that thy profiting may appear to all.

The essence of these words of wisdom is to reveal the mind of God and subsequently hand over to coming generations, inspirational words that will change lives dramatically.

GOD'S THEATRE

What you have in your hand is a book of prophetic meditation that addresses every area of life. These words of wisdom will revitalise your life and mould your destiny in accordance with the plan and purpose of God.

Imagine right now, that you are placed by the Holy Spirit in God's operating theatre. Every word of wisdom is a divine scalpel sent to rip open certain deep aspects of your life. The Holy Spirit is the Surgeon and your life is on God's operating table for a total surgical operation.

THE MAKING OF CHAMPIONS

As the Holy Spirit ministers to you, you must not forget the prayer points at the end of each word of wisdom. By the time God is through with the process of operation, you will come out renewed, revived, revitalise and completely radicalised. Then you will become God's battle-axe and a terror to the kingdom of darkness.

I welcome you into the greatest theatre in the universe; a place where champions are made.

CHAPTER ONE

IF YOU CANNOT WALK ON WATER, DON'T ROCK THE BOAT

Psalms 78:2
I will open my mouth in a parable: I will utter dark sayings of old:

2 Corinthian 11:23-28
Are they ministers of Christ? (I speak as a fool) I am more; in labours more abundant, in stripes above measure, in prisons more frequent, in deaths oft. Of the Jews five times received I forty stripes save one. Thrice was I beaten with rods, once was I stoned, thrice I suffered shipwreck, a night and a day I have been in the deep; In journeyings often, in perils of waters, in perils of robbers, in perils by mine own countrymen, in perils by the heathen, in perils in the city, in perils in the wilderness, in perils in the sea, in perils among false brethren; In weariness and painfulness, in watchings often, in hunger and thirst, in fastings often, in cold and nakedness. Beside those things that are without, that which cometh upon me daily, the care of all the churches.

A man named Daniel read the book of Daniel in the Bible. When he got to the sixth chapter, he read how the biblical Daniel was thrown into the lion's den and he decided to pay a visit to the zoo at the University of Ibadan, Nigeria. When he got there, he jumped into the cage of the lion. The lion, at first ran away because it was not used to people jumping inside its cage. When the instinct of the lion returned, the lion pounced upon and tore Mr. Daniel to pieces.

This was a man that did not know anything about warfare. He probably had never in his life killed a serpent or even a rat but he attempted to fight a lion. Before David could challenge Goliath, he had a testimony that he killed a bear and a lion, but this man had no such testimony, but decided to go and fight a lion.

Saul said to David, "You do not have what it takes and you want to go and fight Goliath who had been a great warrior all his life." David replied that while he was keeping his father's flock, a lion came to pick one of the sheep and he tore it into pieces. He added that he did the same to a bear that attempted it. (Samuel 17:33-36) This shows that David had a convincing CV.

Life is in stages. No one can begin the journey of

life from the final destination. If you start with the most difficult project, you might fail. However, you can attempt the most difficult project after you have succeeded in handling simpler ones. Nobody can attain success with a sudden flight. You need to go a step at a time.

If you are an amateur, as far as walking on water is concerned, do not attempt riding in a boat on the sea. You must garner enough experience if you want to handle more challenging things in life.

If you cannot walk on water, you are likely to rock the boat. If you were never a servant, you cannot become a master. You cannot mentor others, if you were never mentored. You need to have passed through the school of experience if you must demonstrate maturity. Do not ever claim to be whom you are not. Spend adequate time making preparations if you want to achieve greatness in the future. You need an extraordinary CV if you want to be admitted into the hall of extraordinary men and women. You must take one step at a time and avoid jumping the gun. This presupposes that you must spend time to adequately prepare yourself.

Men and women who are celebrated today made great sacrifices in the past. They spent time serving, working tirelessly and paying their dues. It is the wise who prepares for the rainy day. If your preparation is poor, you will end up with a poor result.

May God give you wisdom, may you learn what it takes to be ranked among extraordinary men and women.

Prayer Points:

1. Power for effective development in my calling, come upon me now, in the name of Jesus.

2. I refuse to tarry in the valley of powerlessness, in the name of Jesus.

3. I declare war on spiritual ignorance, in Jesus' name.

4. Oh Lord, ignite my calling with your fire, in the name of Jesus.

5. Oh Lord, let the anointing to excel in my

spiritual and physical life fall on me, in Jesus' name.

6. Oh Lord, enrich me with your gifts, in the name of Jesus.

7. Lord Jesus, work freely in me and through me, in the name of Jesus.

CHAPTER TWO

GOOD LISTENERS
MAKE GOOD PREACHERS

Isaiah 51:1:
Hearken to me, ye that follow after righteousness, ye that seek the LORD: look unto the rock whence ye are hewn, and to the hole of the pit whence ye are digged.

Isaiah 8:20:
To the law and to the testimony: if they speak not according to this word, it is because there is no light in them.

If you see an impatient man who does not listen to anybody, that man cannot make a good preacher. One of the most fantastic preachers I think God has ever sent to this earth was a man called Derek Prince. I thank God for the life of Derek Prince. If not for him, there will be no one who would be bold enough to take up deliverance ministry.

A Cambridge university graduate and highly educated, he started the talk about deliverance. He did not start just like that. One day, he asked the keyboardist to give him an introductory song at a meeting, but the man began to manifest strangely and Derek Prince asked, "Why?" That was how he started a deliverance ministry.

If you want people to listen to you, you must take time to listen to others. If you want to command attention, you must be attentive. If you want to command respect in the future, you must respect those whom God has placed above you now. The sacrifices of today will earn you great recognition and respect in the future. If you are a poor listener, you can never make a good preacher. Excellent listeners are the best communicators. When you listen patiently and analyse what is being said meticulously, when you stand up to speak, your word will draw great attention.

It amazes me when there are believers who are not ready to listen to anyone because they know it all. No matter how poor your knowledge is, nobody will discover how shallow you are if you form the habit of listening patiently. I have come to realise that the best preachers of today are those who took time to listen yesterday. Show me a generation of people who are not ready to listen, and I will show you a generation of people who will become poor, shallow and ineffective preachers.

When the word of God is being preached and there are men and women who are absent-minded or people who are busy with useless activities, such people may never come up as good preachers. Those who do not know that they need thorough knowledge of the word of God will either doze off or give in to distractions when the word of God is being preached. If you want to become a super preacher in the years ahead, you must be a super listener today. When you are attentive, you will acquire the ingredients of effective preaching and ministration.

If you are a poor listener, you will automatically become a poor preacher. Unless you are sensitive to the voice of the Holy Spirit, you will not be able to carry out effective ministry. If you are full of yourself, the Holy Spirit may not be able to impart the gifts of God upon you. Great preachers that have emerged in this generation are men who took time to listen to the voice of the Holy Spirit and accepted the leading of the Lord.

Many preachers who would have become blessings to their generation have ended up as empty shells simply because they paid unnecessary attention to their certificates or academic training. I thank God for brilliant scholars who humbled themselves and allowed God to use them to pioneer revivals and evangelism. Some of these men of God could have decided to retain their pride, but they let go and allowed God to have His way.

Prayer Points:

1. Holy Ghost, breathe on me now, in the name of Jesus.

2. Oh Lord, produce in me the power of self-control and gentleness, in the name of Jesus.

3. Oh Lord, teach me to die to self, in Jesus' name.

4. The anointing to be a good listener, fall upon me now, in the name of Jesus.

5. My father, help me to listen to your voice everyday, in Jesus' name.

CHAPTER THREE

THE MORE OPEN YOUR MOUTH IS, THE SHALLOW YOUR MIND

Proverbs 4:23

Keep thy heart with all diligence; for out of it are the issues of life.

Matthew 12:34

O generation of vipers, how can ye, being evil, speak good things? For out of the abundance of the heart the mouth speaketh.

If you see someone talking 200 words per minute, he is a candidate for a deliverance session. When you talk too much, you are prone to mistakenly say something that you are not supposed to say, or talk yourself out of God's blessings for your life. God is not a talkative.

There is a wide gap between the power of the mind and the power of the mouth. Great minds are not great talkers. When your mind is deep, you cannot find anytime for gossip. Empty and shallow minds are incurable gossips. When your mind is filled with good virtues, you will not open your mouth at random. You need a mind that is controlled by the Holy Spirit, if you do not want to experience what can be described as verbal diarrhea. If you allow the Holy Spirit to take charge of your life, you will not become loud-mouthed. Great men and women are not talkatives. When you are a stranger to the economy of words, it shows that your heart has nothing to offer. Empty barrels make the most noise. When your mind is full of matter, your mouth will reveal very little.

Those who talk like parrots can only boost of quantity, not quality. If you do not allow the ray of divine light to permeate your heart, your mouth will utter unsavoury words. The quality of your mind is known by the kind of words that come out from your mouth. If your mind is solid, you will speak solid words. If your mind is scattered, your words will distribute viruses.

You need a mind that is charged by fire. If you must speak fiery words, you need to seriously work on the materials which you allow to fill or dominate your thoughts. If you want your words to carry weight, you need wisdom.

When words are spoken without caution, it shows that the mind of the speaker is on riot. Work on your mind and you will not need to remember the words you have spoken. With the fountain of an anointed mind, the mouth will become an outlet that gives out words that are seasoned with grace.

You must allow the Holy Spirit to incubate your life, if you want to produce inspirational words that will impact destinies.

Prayer Points:

1. Oh Lord, keep a watch over the door of my mouth, in the name of Jesus.

2. Let the words of my mouth and the meditation of my heart be acceptable in your sight Lord, in the name of Jesus.

3. Power to exercise control over my mouth, fall upon me now, in the name of Jesus.

4. Mouth diarrhea, loose your hold over my life, in the name of Jesus.

5. I receive the spirit of self-control over my mouth, in Jesus' name.

6. Oh Lord, deliver me from the natural darkness of my mind, in Jesus' name.

CHAPTER FOUR

NO MAN IS FREE WHO IS NOT A MASTER OF HIMSELF

Galatians 5:22-25

But the fruit of the Spirit is love, joy, peace, longsuffering, gentleness, goodness, faith, meekness, temperance: against such there is no law. And they that are Christ's have crucified the flesh with the affections and lusts. If we live in the Spirit, let us also walk in the Spirit.

If you cannot master yourself, you are in bondage. Your freedom begins when you attain the mastery of yourself. Without inner control, there cannot be any form of stability. To be free, you must exercise restraint. If you cannot tame yourself, your life will be in shambles. You must get to a point when checks are exercised and your life is completely streamlined according to divine purpose.

Freedom can only be found when the flesh is under control. A man or a woman who has lost control of his taste, desire and value is under serious bondage. If carnality or the flesh has mastered you, you are a slave and not a master.

You must be ready to place your life under the control of the Holy Spirit if you want true freedom. You must obtain freedom at all cost by placing your desires and appetites under close scrutiny and control.

Prayer Points:

1.   Every internal bondage magnetising external bondage, be broken, in the name of Jesus.

2.   I release myself from every evil domination and control, in the name of Jesus.

3.   By Your rulership, oh Lord, let the lust of the flesh in my life die, in Jesus' name.

4.   Lord, help me to identify and deal with any weakness in me that can hinder the manifestation of my miracles, in the name of Jesus.

5.   I release myself from any inherited bondage, in the name of Jesus.

CHAPTER FIVE

YOU ATTRACT AND KEEP PEOPLE BY THE QUALITIES YOU DISPLAY AND POSSESS

1 Corinthian 4:16
Wherefore I beseech you, be ye followers of me.

1 Corinthian 11:1
Be ye followers of me, even as I also am of Christ.

If you see a fellowship that is not growing, look at the pastor. Your inner qualities and your outward manifestations will either attract or repel those around you. If your life is loaded with positive qualities, you will attract people who appreciate those qualities. If there are negative qualities in your life, people will be repelled. If you want to groom disciples who are godly, you must manifest godly principles. Your character will magnetise or repel those around you.

If you lack good qualities, you will lack sincere followership. But, if your life is an embodiment of godly virtues and excellence, you will discover that people will swarm around you, and your company will be desired. Your influence will be appreciated and your quality will lead people heaven-ward. In the first place, you cannot attract people when your character and conduct leave much to be desired. It is even possible sometimes for people to be mistakenly attracted.

But, keeping them would be difficult.

People can mistakenly come around, but there is no way you can keep them when the qualities you possess are below standard. Maintain good qualities and you will not need to coerce people to become loyal to you. Loyalty is a substance of good qualities. As a leader when you have positive qualities, people will be attracted to you and they will display the highest quality of loyalty. If a leader begins to lose his impact, it is because he has lost the quality that endears people to him. If you lack good qualities, look inward today and begin to build qualities that will make people to keep milling around you.

Prayer Points:

1. Oh Lord, let me study and stand for discipline, in the name of Jesus.

2. Oh Lord, give me deeper knowledge of You, in the name of Jesus.

3. Lord, give me power in private prayer, in the name of Jesus.

4. Oh God, come as a Teacher, and fill me with

all understanding, in the name of Jesus.

5.   I declare that I shall not grieve or resist the Holy Spirit, in the name of Jesus.

CHAPTER SIX

TO GET THE RIGHT ANSWER, YOU MUST ASK THE RIGHT QUESTION

Ecclesiastes 10:15

The labour of the foolish wearieth every one of them, because he knoweth not how to go to the city.

Even when talking to heaven, you must ask the right questions. The type of question you ask will determine the kind of answers you will get. Wrong questions will attract wrong answers. If your perspective is wrong, what you will discover will be wrong. Your attitude determines the type of results you will get. When you work on your approach, you will end up with an achievement that is positive.

Do not expect the right answers to your questions, if your approach is wrong. If you want to come with good results, you must follow a pathway that is not prone to errors in any way. When it comes to things of the kingdom, your approach must be positive, if you want to arrive at the right destination.

Prayer Points:

1. Anointing for excellence, fall upon me, in the name of Jesus.

2.   I receive fresh fire and anointing, in the name of Jesus.

3.   Lord Jesus, increase daily in my life, in Jesus' name.

4.   Lord Jesus, maintain Your gifts in my life, in the name of Jesus.

5.   Holy Spirit, inflame and fire my heart, in the name of Jesus.

CHAPTER SEVEN

SIMPLE THINGS BECOME COMPLEX WHEN YOU DO NOT FOLLOW ADVICE

Proverbs 15:22

Without counsel, purposes are disappointed; but in the multitude of counsellors they are established.

Hebrews 8:5

Who serve unto the example and shadow of heavenly things, as Moses was admonished of God when he was about to make the tabernacle: for, See, saith he, that thou make all things according to the pattern shewed to thee in the mount.

There is nothing as good as following sound advice. When you keep to the instructions given to you, complex things will become simple. Those who are self-opinionated find things difficult. When such people refuse to follow good advice, things that are simple become complex.

No man is an island; complete in himself. You need the counsel and advice of wise men and women around you. If only you can learn how to extract wise counsel from those who are ahead of you, you will find it easy to achieve and fulfil your destiny.

Life is simple. You can achieve your goals with ease when you learn to follow sound advice.

Prayer Points:

1. You my life, hear the word of the Lord, you shall not follow the counsel of evil counsellors, in the name of Jesus.

2. Power to discern and follow good counsel, fall upon me now, in the name of Jesus.

3. My life, receive divine counsel, in the name of Jesus.

4. Oh God my father, surround my life with good counsellors that will help me to get my destination, in the name of Jesus.

5. I shall not fall into the errors of my ancestors, in the name of Jesus.

6. Let the wisdom of God to take right decisions fall upon me, in the name of Jesus.

CHAPTER EIGHT

IF YOU ARE NOT BENEFICIAL TO OTHERS, YOUR DEATH WILL NOT BE A LOSS TO ANYBODY

Psalms 37:37
Mark the perfect man, and behold the upright: for the end of that man is peace.

If you live a life of no benefit, if you die nobody will cry: No value will be attached to you when you are no more. However, if your life is filled with great values, you will be missed when you are no more. If you are selfish and your life is devoid of impact, when you die, people will heave a sigh of relief. Rather than mourn your death, people will express happiness because you are no longer around.

A life of impact will make you irreplaceable. But when those who are around derive no benefit whatsoever from your presence, your death or absence will mean nothing to them. You need to look inward and examine the level of impact your life has over people. Life has value only when you live for others rather than live for yourself. You must empty your life and be a channel of blessing to the young and to the old. Let those who come across you derive benefits that will make them miss you when death comes.

Prayer Points:

1. Power to make positive impact in my generation, fall on me, in Jesus' name.

2. I shall not be a waste to my generation, in the name of Jesus.

3. Lord, let my generation celebrate me, in the name of Jesus.

4. Oh God my father, rekindle the fire of charity in me, in the name of Jesus.

CHAPTER NINE

THE WORLD HAS ENACTED 35 MILLION LAWS, JUST TO ENFORCE THE TEN COMMANDMENTS

Isaiah 8:20

To the law and to the testimony: if they speak not according to this word, it is because there is no light in them.

Isaiah 8:16

Bind up the testimony, seal the law among my disciples.

Galatians 5:22-23

But the fruit of the spirit is love, joy, peace, longsuffering, gentleness, goodness, faith, meekness, temperance; against such there is no law.

There are over 35 million laws in the world. All these are offshoots or corollaries of the Ten Commandments in the Bible. Our life is still guided by the Ten Commandments.

When you obey the word of God, you will not need to worry about human laws. The truth is that, international laws, national laws, ceremonial laws, religious laws, business laws, customary laws and laws that control human interactions are all taken from the word of God. The Ten Commandments has given birth to over 35 million laws. This laws have become very complex. The world is gradually coming to terms with the fact that those who obey the ten commandments of the Bible will not break human laws.

Beloved, you may not know the details of the over 35 million laws that had been enacted in the world today. But, when you know God and you follow the commandment of the Bible, you will be living above the level of millions of laws that are being enacted by men and women all over the world.

Prayer Points:

1. Power to listen to the word of God at all times, fall upon me now, in the name of Jesus.

2. Confusion of this generation, my life is not for you, die, in the name of Jesus.

3. I have the mind of Christ, therefore I shall not be tosses around by false doctrine, in the name of Jesus.

4. I walk in the liberty of the word of God in Christ Jesus, in the mighty name of Jesus.

CHAPTER TEN

NOTHING IS ABSOLUTELY FREE IN LIFE

I Chronicles 29:5
The gold for things of gold, and the silver for things of silver, and for all manner of work to be made by the hands of artificers. And who then is willing to consecrate his service this day unto the LORD?

You must let go of one thing to gain something greater. If you are a fisherman, you must lose a worm to gain a fish. The law of give-and-take is in operation all over the world.

The truth about life is that, in life you lose some and gain some. Nothing is free. There is really no free lunch anywhere. To get, you must give. To gain, you must make sacrifices. To achieve your goals, you must give whatever it takes. To get to the top, you must be ready to climb the ladder. To obtain the gifts of God, you must give time and attention to the things of God. Nothing is totally free. If you want to grow spiritually, you must be ready to sacrifice your leisure and whatever appeals to the flesh. You must pay a price to obtain the prize. If you want to gain the next level, you must be ready to lose recognition at this level. If you want to be applauded, you must be ready to receive abusive words as a result of your goals in life. As far as excellence is concerned, the rule is: nothing ventured, nothing gained.

Prayer Points:

1. I receive power to pay the price for spiritual growth, in the name of Jesus.

2. Oh God, give me deeper power in private prayers, in Jesus' name.

3. Lord, give me a deeper knowledge of Thyself, in Jesus' name..

CHAPTER ELEVEN

DO NOT MAKE SOMEBODY A PRIORITY IN YOUR LIFE, WHEN THEY ARE MAKING YOU AN OPTION

Galatians 6:7

Be not deceived; God is not mocked: for whatsoever a man soweth, that shall he also reap.

You need wisdom when you relate with neighbours, colleagues and friends. The law of sowing and reaping is a powerful law. There are times to pay people back in their own coins. If somebody is not ready to accord you recognition, you are free to move to where your value will be appreciated. Never make anyone a priority who is not ready to make you a priority.

You do not owe anyone recognition who is not ready to recognise you. You can step aside and move away from where you are tolerated to where you are celebrated. If someone will not make you a priority, make him or her a mere option. Do not give your best to anyone who is not ready to offer you his or her best. Do not keep all your eggs in a basket, and give it not to someone who closes his or her eyes, and likely to break all of them at a go.

It is often wise to treat people the way they have decided to treat you. Do not impose yourself on those who are fed up with you.

Prayer Points:

1. I receive the grace to choose the right friends, in the name of Jesus.

2. My destiny helpers, locate me by fire, in the name of Jesus.

3. Oh Lord my father, deliver me from unfriendly friends, in the name of Jesus.

CHAPTER TWELVE

NO ONE CAN DISRESPECT YOU WITHOUT YOUR PERMISSION

Job 29:8
The young men saw me, and hid themselves: and the aged arose, and stood up.

You can refuse to be disrespected. No one on earth has the capability to disgrace you. The kind of disrespect or disgrace you receive is the type you decide to accept. What you tolerate is what people will give to you. If you choose to make your life a trash bin, people will drop their refuse and treat you like rags.

You have the right to say no to any attempt to ridicule or disrespect you. You have the right to permit or refuse any form to intimidation or ridicule. When you rise up and bluntly say no, those who want to rubbish you will stay clear. You are the only one who can allow or disallow insults and reproaches. When you keep your dignity, people will be left with no option than to respect you. Nobody has the licence to disgrace you unless you decide to grant the licence.

Prayer Points:

1.   Power to see myself the way God sees me, come upon me now, in the name of Jesus.

2.   Oh God, be the glory and the lifter of my head, in the name of Jesus.

CHAPTER THIRTEEN

NO ONE IS SO DEAF AS THOSE WHO WILL NOT LISTEN

Matthew 13:9
Who hath ears to hear, let him hear.

Revelation 3:6
He that hath an ear, let him hear what the Spirit saith unto the churches.

Anyone who refuses to listen is as good as deaf. When you listen you will be saved from trouble. If you listen for five minutes, it can save you five years of crisis. To refuse to listen is to become as deaf as those who cannot hear anything whatsoever. Those who are not ready to listen can be likened to the deaf dog that cannot hear the hunter's whistle.

When you get to a point when you no longer listen to pieces of advice or instruction, you are deaf. You may not know when danger is near. Those who refuse to follow directions are in the company of the deaf. Such people can walk into traps without knowing that they are stepping into trouble. You need to fight against whatever and whosoever is telling you not to listen. A good listener will not face the dangers experienced by the deaf. The moment you stop listening, you have become as endangered as the deaf who can no longer hear warning signals. May God continue to speak to you, and may you continue to listen to the voice of the Holy Spirit.

Prayer Points:

1.   I receive the anointing to be sensitive to the voice of the Holy Spirit, in the name of Jesus.

2.   Lord, revive me in the inner man, in the name of Jesus.

3.   My father, give the spirit of discernment, in Jesus' name.

4.   Oh Lord, help me to be still and quiet in your presence, in the name of Jesus.

5.   I shall not be deaf and dumb in the spirit, in the name of Jesus.

6.   Any trait of a bat in my spiritual life, die, in the name of Jesus.

CHAPTER FOURTEEN

YOU DESERVE WHAT YOU TOLERATE

James 4:7

Submit yourselves therefore to God. Resist the devil, and he will flee from you.

If you tolerate the enemy, then you deserve whatever the enemy does to you. The devil does not have the right to harass you. The harassment you allow is the one you will suffer. If you tolerate satanic attacks, you actually deserve those attacks. The enemy does not have the right to subject you to wickedness and torture. When you tolerate the wickedness of the enemy you will remain a punching bag that will be battered continuously. You cannot afford to allow the enemy to play you back and forth like a ball.

If you are a constant victim of wickedness and harassment, it is because you have allowed and tolerated those things. If you do not demonstrate zero tolerance towards the enemy, you have no one else to blame but yourself.

Prayer Points:

1. I shall laugh my enemies to scorn after the order of Elijah, in the name of Jesus.

2.	The enemy will not have dominion over me again, in the name of Jesus.

3.	I recover all my lost breakthrough from the camp of the enemy, in Jesus' name.

4.	I repossess my lost ground in seven-folds, in the name of Jesus.

5.	I will not surrender to the enemy, in the name of Jesus.

CHAPTER FIFTEEN

YOU CANNOT ENSLAVE A
BIBLE READER

1 Timothy 4:15

Meditate upon these things; give thyself wholly to them; that thy profiting may appear to all.

The nations where the Bible is their foundation are the greatest nations in the world. Bible readers are hard to enslave. Men and women who know the truth cannot be placed under bondage. Those who live under the dazzling light of the word of God cannot suffer what is characteristic of those who live in darkness.

As long as you remain a Bible reader, the devil will not be able to take you into any form of slave-camp. It is indeed true that if you are not informed, you will be deformed. If you are not a good reader of the Bible, you will be raided by the army of darkness. When you are an ardent Bible reader, you will not know the shackles of slavery. Those who are under the influence of the Bible cannot be brought into the realm of ignorance. Bible readers cannot be exploited. But, men and women who close their Bibles will suffer all forms of enslavement. The Bible will either keep you from sin or sin will take you away from the Bible.

As long as you are reading the Bible, Satan cannot subject you to the type of ignorance that will turn your life upside down. When you read your Bible, you will remain on top. Elemental forces will not be able to control you. The light of the word of God will drive away any invasion of darkness. Your enemy cannot overcome you when the word of God richly dwells in you.

The more you read your Bible, the more the enemy will find it difficult to lead you astray. As long as you open the Bible and the word of God occupies your heart, the devil will find it difficult to subject you to any form of bondage. When you read the Bible more and more, you will be free and be free indeed.

The knowledge of the Bible will make you too strong to be enslaved by the enemy.

Prayer Points:

1.   Oh God, come as light, and illuminate the Scriptures unto me, in the name of Jesus.

2.   My father, let me hunger and thirst for

Your word daily, in the name of Jesus.

3. Take me deeper in the school of the word of God, oh Lord, in the name of Jesus.

CHAPTER SIXTEEN

BACKSLIDING BEGINS ON THE KNEES

Hebrews 12:12

Wherefore lift up the hands which hang down, and the feeble knees:

It is when your knees of prayer fail, that backsliding starts. Weakness in prayer will automatically translate to a weak life. A weak prayer altar is an indication of the fact that you have gone so far away from the Lord. Backslidden men and women often starts the downwards journey with their knees.

When your knees are becoming weak, your spiritual life will experience a short power voltage. Any power that succeeds in affecting your prayer life is out to make you a slave.

Your knees are your greatest source of strength. Strong knees will strengthen your life. Weakness in your knees will weaken your life. When your knees are wobbly at the altar of prayer, you will begin to experience internal weakness. You need revived knees in order to experience a revived life.

Failure begins when your knees are feeble. Prayerlessness is the beginning of backsliding. When your knees are no longer bowed at the altar of prayers, sooner or later, backsliding will become inevitable. You will begin to find it difficult to tarry in prayer. Therefore, watch over your knees and you will discover that is the source of your strength. To stop backsliding, you must not allow anything to tamper with your prayer altar.

Prayer Points:

1. Every power waging war against my prayer life, die, in the name of Jesus.

2. Oh God, empower me to win the battle against sleep, in the name of Jesus.

3. My prayer altar, receive the fire of revival, in Jesus' name.

4. Holy Ghost fire, incubate my prayer life, in the name of Jesus.

5. I refuse to retire, I shall refire, in Jesus' name.

6. Every spirit slumber, I bury you today, in Jesus' name.

CHAPTER SEVENTEEN

SIN IS A SHORT WORD THAT SHORTENS LIFE

I John 5:16

If any man see his brother sin a sin which is not unto death, he shall ask, and he shall give him life for them that sin not unto death. There is a sin unto death: I do not say that he shall pray for it.

Although sin is a three-letter word, it has a capacity for shortening human lives. When you allow sin to have an inroad into your life, you have inadvertently allowed your life to be shortened. The more you give yourself to sin, the more you are responsible for a shortened lifespan.

Just a little sin is enough to shorten your life. What people do for a very short period can cut their life short. Nothing cuts human life short like sin. Those who allow sin in their lives will end up with shortened lives.

Holiness will prolong your life. When you live a life that is holy, you will be healthy. Holiness will increase your days on earth. No wonder the Bible says fools make a mockery of sin.

If you want to prolong your days on earth, and if your utmost desire are days of heaven on earth, you must avoid sin like a plague. When you are holy within and without, your health will be radiant and your days on earth will increase.

Whenever you are tempted, you must not lose sight of the fact that sin shortens life. Embrace holiness and live long. Allow sin to multiply in your life and you stand the risk of untimely death. You need to keep away sin so that sin will not terminate your life unexpectedly.

Prayer Points:

1. Lord, deliver me from the daily snare that are assigned against me, in the name of Jesus.

2. I bind the spirit of sexual immorality, in Jesus' name.

3. I will not mortgage my calling on the lap of Delilah and Jezebel, in the name of Jesus.

4. I shall not be a missed fired arrow in the hands of my Maker, in the name of Jesus.

5. Oh glory of my calling, arise and shine, in the name of Jesus.

CHAPTER EIGHTEEN

IF YOU CANNOT BE DISCOURAGED, YOU CONFUSE THE DEVIL

1 Kings 19:4

But he himself went a day's journey into the wilderness; ad came and sat down under a juniper tree: and he requested for himself that he might die; and said, it is enough; now, O LORD, take away my life; for I am not better than my fathers.

1 Samuel 30:6

and David hath great distress, for the people have said to stone him, for the soul of all the people hath been bitter, each for his sons and for his daughters; and David doth strengthen himself in Lord his God.

To confuse the devil, you must refuse to be discouraged. The devil is in trouble each time you win the battle against discouragement. No matter what happens, you must be courageous and refuse whatever makes you to fall victim of discouragement. You can confuse the enemy through unwavering faith. The devil cannot overcome you as long as you do not yield to discouragement.

It has been discovered that discouragement is one of the devil's toughest tools. No matter what you are going through at the moment, once you keep the fire of encouragement burning, the devil will be left with no option than to flee. You can resist the devil by saying no to discouragement and the devil will flee.

When you draw inner motivation through faith, the devil will be at a loss concerning what to do to win the fight. When you fight the fight of faith on the platform of encouragement, the devil cannot overcome you. You must be a man or woman of faith and encouragement.

Do not allow the voice of the enemy to attach discouragement to your life. As far as God is concerned, there is nothing on earth that can discourage a faithful child who always look up to Him and believes that the impossible is possible.

Prayer Points:

1.   Aries, oh Lord, disappoint my oppressors and cast them down, in the name of Jesus.

2.   Let the joy of the enemy over my life be turned to sorrow, in the mighty name of Jesus.

3.   Spirit of discouragement, loose your hold over my life, in the name of Jesus.

4.   Oh God, arise and make me a mysterious wonder, in the name of Jesus.

5.   Every arrow of sadness and sorrow fired against my life, backfire, in the name of Jesus.

CHAPTER NINETTEN

IF YOU DON'T KNOW WHERE YOU ARE GOING, THEN YOU ARE LOST

Proverbs 28:18

Whoso is walking uprightly is saved: but he that is perverse in his ways shall fall at once.

You must know where you are at the moment. You must also be aware of your final destination.

If you are unaware of where you are heading to, you might not know how to get there. We live in a world where many people are lost. There is no sense of direction. Many people do not know where they are or where they are going.

Are you aware of your goals in life? Do you know what you are meant to achieve? If you do not know your goals, you are lost in the strictest sense of the word. Many do not even know where they are coming from, let alone where they are supposed to be in life.

You must know where you are going. You must have an overview of your final destination and be able to calculate the steps that must be taken before you can get there. If you have no goal or objective, I put it to you that you are lost.

Today, you can retrace your steps and seek the face of God to know where He wants you to be. Once your destination is discovered, you will receive inner motivation to make the journey. Each day you must work towards getting to your destination and in no time, you will achieve your goals and reach it.

Prayer Points:

1. Holy Spirit, be thou my guide in all that I do, in the name of Jesus.

2. Father, help me to be focus in life, in the name of Jesus.

3. Anoint to fulfil my destiny, fall upon me now, in the name of Jesus.

4. Oh God, arise and help me to get to my destination safely, in the name of Jesus.

CHAPTER TWENTY

IT IS POSSIBLE TO ENTERNTAIN DEMONS AS WELL AS ANGELS UNAWARES!

Hebrews 13:2

Be not forgetful to entertain strangers: for thereby some have entertained angels unawares.

May you not entertain demons unawares. Your conduct and activities will either glorify God or gladden the heart of Satan. What you do will either make angels in heaven to rejoice or make demons excited.

While it is possible to entertain angels unawares, it is also possible to entertain demons unawares. Do you want to entertain angels or demons? You can choose to make demons angry.

May God help you not to entertain demons. May your conduct never provoke a party in the demonic headquarters. May God sentence you to a lifestyle of conduct that will cause jubilations in heaven. May your life make demons hiss and sorrowful continually.

Prayer Points:

1. Oh Lord, create in me a clean heart by Your power, in the name of Jesus.

2.   Oh Lord, give me the eyes of Elisha and the ears of Samuel, in the name of Jesus.

3.   Anything in my life attracting evil presence, come out and die, in the name of Jesus.

4.   Mark of the wicked in my body, be wiped off, in the name of Jesus.

5.   Blood of Jesus, purify my body, soul and spirit, in the name of Jesus.

CHAPTER TWENTY - ONE

IF YOU DO NOT FIGHT, YOU CANNOT CONQUER

1 Timothy 6:12

Fight the good fight of faith, lay hold on eternal life, whereunto thou art also called, and hath professed a good profession before many witnesses.

L ife is a battle and warfare is inevitable. There is no victory without warfare.

You cannot celebrate without fighting the battles of life. If you avoid battles, you are making conquest or victory impossible. Those who run away from the battle-field cannot wear the crown of victory. Failure to fight is failure to overcome. You cannot conquer an enemy that you refuse to fight.

To be promoted to the next level, you must fight and overcome every opposition at your present level. He who will be valiant must of necessity fight the good fight of faith.

You must do all the fighting today, if you must earn and celebrate victory tomorrow. Run away from the field of battle and you will not be classified among the overcomers or victors in life.

Prayer Points:

1. Every Goliath boasting against my breakthroughs, die, in the name of Jesus.

2. I decree against serpent and scorpion, let their poison die, in the name of Jesus.

3. Let the wickedness of the wicked come an end, in the name of Jesus.

4. Every enchantment assigned for my downfall, die, in the name of Jesus.

5. Any personality carrying the seed of wickedness against my life, be exposed and be disgraced, in the name of Jesus.

CHAPTER TWENTY - TWO

FLIES DO NOT PERCH ON A HOT POT: IF YOU ARE ON FIRE, CERTAIN THINGS CANNOT HAPPEN TO YOU

Isaiah 64:2

As when the melting fire burneth, the fire causeth the waters to boil, to make thy name known to thine adversaries. That the nations may tremble at thy presence!

If you are cold or lukewarm, elemental forces will continue to harass you. Rats, lizards or other animals do not play with fire. Pest and insects cannot carry out their sports in a location that is ablaze with fire. Flies will stay away.

Nauseating circumstances cannot come to the precincts of those who are on fire for God. The devil cannot mess up with you if you are truly on fire for God. When fire falls upon you, 'strangers' will be frightened out of their closed places.

You are constantly harassed by funny powers because you lack enough power. No power can decide to touch a mighty conflagration of fire. If there are too many flies buzzing around your ears, spiritually speaking, it simply shows that your fire is not enough.

The moment your entire life is set on fire,

demons will declare you too hot to handle. Rather than confront you, they will bow. When workers of darkness discover that they cannot confront your fire-power, they will rather confess or they will surreptitiously bow to you knowing that they have failed.

To get rid of nauseating flies, be on fire for God.

Prayer Points:

1. My life, be too hot for the enemy to handle, in the name of Jesus.

2. Holy Ghost, turn me to fire, in the name of Jesus.

3. My inner man, receive fire, in the name of Jesus.

4. My prayer altar, catch the fire of the Holy Ghost.

5. Holy Ghost, ignite me to the glory of God, in the name of Jesus.

CHAPTER TWENTY - THREE

IF YOU MAKE YOURSELF A MOUSE, THE CAT WILL CATCH YOU

Daniel 7:21
'I behold, and the same horn made war with the saints, and prevailed against them.

Revelation 13:7
And it was given unto him to make war with the saints, and to overcome them: and power was given him over all kindreds, and tongues, and nations.

The way you dress is the way you will be addressed. Your general comportment will either attract insults or respect. If you mimic the cry of a mouse, a cat will pounce on you. If you manifest the mentality of a mouse, cats will locate you.

It is the spirit of the mouse in you that will attract all kinds of funny cats. If the influence of the Lion of the tribe of Judah is strong in you, cats will be frightened away.

Never reduce yourself to a mouse. If you do, you will become mincemeat for every cat around you. When you upgrade your life and destiny, and you are no longer in the class of vulnerable mice, no cat will mess around with you.

A believer who carried himself or herself like a

mouse will be tormented by every wicked cat around.

Prayer Points:

1. Lord, contend with them that contend with me, in the name of Jesus.

2. Oh God, dash the power of stubborn pursuers in pieces like a potter's vessel, in the name of Jesus.

3. Arise, oh Lord, and lift up thine arm in war, in the name of Jesus.

4. Oh Lord, break my enemies with Your rod of iron, in the name of Jesus.

5. Oh Lord, barricade me from the wicked that oppress me, in the name of Jesus.

CHAPTER TWENTY - FOUR

IF YOU STAND NEUTRAL, THEN YOU STAND FOR NOTHING

Psalms 26:11
But as for me, I will walk in mine integrity! redeem me, and be merciful unto me.

Psalms 51:6
Behold, thou desired truth in the inward parts: and in the hidden part thou shalt make me to know wisdom.

You must stand for something if you want to be outstanding in life. Those who sit on the fence will fall flat on their faces when the fence collapses.

If you stand for nothing, you will be regarded as someone who amounts to nothing.

Do not be neutral. Avoid the average lifestyle. Be known for something. Let there be no doubt in the heart of anyone concerning where you truly belong.

Do not be found among those who have no identity whatsoever. If you stand for nothing when the headcount is done, you will be classified as belonging nowhere. Carve out an identity. Let the whole world know where you stand. Be bold; be committed. Do not be afraid of taking your stand for Christ.

Dare to stand out. Dare to be like Daniel. This is what it takes to be outstanding.

Prayer Points:

1. I shall not warm myself with the fire of the enemy, in the name of Jesus.

2. Power to stand for truth and righteousness, fall upon me now, in Jesus' name.

3. My father, give me the grace to declare my stand for You anywhere I find myself, in the name of Jesus.

4. I shall not deny my savior when it matters most, in the name of Jesus.

5. Power as of old, fall upon me now, in the name of Jesus.

CHAPTER TWENTY- FIVE

THE NATIONAL ANTHEM OF HELL FIRE IS: "EVERYONE IS DOING IT"

Proverbs 11:21

Though hand join in hand, the wicked shall not be unpunished: but the seed of the righteous shall be delivered.

H ell has an anthem. The hit song is: "everyone is doing it." When you are invited to jump on the bandwagon, it is a clever invitation to hell. One of the biggest lie from the pit of hell is: "do not worry, everybody is doing it."

Beloved, the fact that everybody is doing it does nothing to change anything. The fact that majority can be found on a particular lane does not make the lane the right lane. The fact that majority is involved in the rat race does not justify the final destination. When you find that everybody is doing a particular thing, take caution; there might be danger.

Do not listen to those who tell you that everybody cannot be wrong. Beloved, even if the majority is on the wrong track, God will never change His standard. Remember, the broad way can accommodate anyone: the narrow way can only accommodate very few. Do not be part of the majority. Choose to be different.

Prayer Points:

1. Oh God my father, give me the grace to follow You to the end, in the name of Jesus.

2. Strength of God, empower me, in the name of Jesus.

3. Oh God of Elijah, arise and give me the mantle of fire, in Jesus' name.

4. Every weapon, fashioned against my high calling, be destroyed, in the name of Jesus.

5. Oh glory of my calling, arise and shine , in the name of Jesus.

CHAPTER TWENTY- SIX

FORCE YOURSELF TO PRAY, BEFORE YOU ARE FORCED TO PRAY

Psalms 65:2

O thou that hearest prayer, unto thee shall all flesh come.

Prayer is your only weapon for survival. Your victory in life is determined by your prayer level. Do not face crisis only to discover that you are not sufficiently prepared because of your weak prayer life. Avoid emergency prayer. Pray before an emergency, so that emergency will not force you to pray.

In the time of peace, prepare for war. You must force yourself to pray before you are forced to pray by situations and circumstances. The best preparation you can make in life is to pray adequately before you find yourself in a situation that requires adequate prayer. When you pray enough, there will be no fear in your heart when a challenge comes up.

Most of the time, it is not easy to pray during an emergency. You must pray now so that you will not be looking askance for how to pray when you are harassed with negative circumstances.

Prayer Points:

1. Prayer power, come upon me now, in the name of Jesus.

2. I refuse to tarry in the valley of powerlessness, in the name of Jesus.

3. Eagle of my calling shall mount up by the power in the blood of Jesus.

4. Power to prevail in the place of prayer, fall on me now, in the name of Jesus.

5. I soak myself in the blood of Jesus.

CHAPTER TWENTY- SEVEN

IT IS NOT HARD TO TELL A LIE, BUT IT IS HARD TO TELL ONLY ONE LIE

Psalms 58:3

The wicked are estranged from the womb: they go astray as soon as they be born, speaking lies.

A single lie is never enough, you will need to tell more lies if you must establish the lies you have already told. No lie exists in isolation. A lie is such a negative thing that additional ones are always required to cover up the previous one.

When you tell a lie, you will either need to go back and own up to the fact that you have told a lie, or you must go on as a student in the school of liars and manufacture new lies in order to cover up your track.

I am yet to see a liar who can boldly rise up and declare that he or she has told only one lie. Those who have become incurable liars today probably thought that they could tell only one lie and stop. No lie is safe to tell. It is a journey that has no specific destination. If you are used to telling lies, you will discover, sooner or later, that it is hard to tell a single lie.

The safest thing to do is to keep your lips from lying. The moment you decide to tell a lie, other lies will be attracted.

Prayer Points:

1.   Power to be faithful, come upon my life, in the name of Jesus.

2.   Every spirit of lying in my life, die, in the name of Jesus.

3.   Spring of lie, dry up in my life, in the name of Jesus.

4.   I reject the anointing of Gehazi, in the name of Jesus.

5.   Let the word of God dwell in me richly, in the name of Jesus.

CHAPTER TWENTY- EIGHT

NO ONE CAN LOOK DOWN ON YOU WHEN YOU ARE TALLER THAN THEY ARE

Proverb 12:24

The hand of the diligent shall bear rule: but the slothful shall be under tribute.

What matters in life is the height you have attained. When God takes you to a height that is above and beyond insults, you will enjoy immunity from disgrace.

Do not worry when people try to look down on you. As long as God has placed you above them, their looks will not matter. Rather than complain about people's looks or derogatory remarks, concentrate your effort on how God will lift you up even more.

When God lifts you up, the words and attitudes of scoffers will no longer matter. It is impossible for anyone to look down on you when you are taller than they are. At that point, rather than look down on you, they will be forced to look up to you.

When God has lifted up your head and you tower above your colleagues and contemporaries, you will not need to worry about anybody's look. The only one who can be looked down upon is someone with a short stature, figuratively speaking.

When you go up higher in life, both spiritually and materially, no one will be able to look down on you.

Prayer Points:

1. I bind every spirit intimidating me, in the name of Jesus.

2. The righteous is as bold as a lion, therefore, I receive the spirit of boldness, in the name of Jesus.

3. Spirit of fear, die, in Jesus' name.

4. Oh God, baptise me with the spirit of excellence, in the name of Jesus.

5. My destiny, become excellent, in the name of Jesus.

CHAPTER TWENTY- NINE

GOD SPEAKS TO THOSE WHO LISTEN

Revelation 3:20

Behold, I stand at the door, and knock: if any man hear my voice, and open the door, I will come in to him, and will sup with him, and he with me.

God demonstrates great economy with His words. He only speaks to those with listening ears.

God will not speak to you when your mind is cloudy. He will not speak to you when your heart is filled with personal opinions. God will not send His word to you until He discovers that you are a good listener.

Listening ears attract God's attention. God has something to say if you are ready to listen. God can spend years standing at the door and knocking. He will not utter a word until you decide to open the door of your heart to him.

The Holy Spirit has deep messages for you, but nothing will be uttered while you are busy listening to all types of human voices. Those who are dull of hearing will not hear what the Spirit is saying. It is unfortunate that we live in a generation where people with itchy ears are on the increase.

I put it to you that God will not waste His time to speak to you when you want to hear what catches your fancy only. To hear the voice of the Lord loud and clear, you must be sold out to God, and you must be ready to abide by the perfect will of God.

Do you want to receive God's best? You must be a good listener, and you must be ready to do His absolute will.

Prayer Points:

1.   Oh Lord, help me to listen your voice, in the name of Jesus.

2.   Teach me to be silent in Your presence, oh Lord, in Jesus' name.

3.   I want the fire that is fresh in my life, in the name of Jesus.

4.   Power to mount up with wings as eagles, come on me, in the name of Jesus.

CHAPTER THIRTY

SLUMBERING SAINTS SERVE SATAN

Matthew 25:3-12

They that were foolish took their lamps, and took no oil with them: But the wise took oil in their vessels with their lamps. While the bridegroom tarried, they all slumbered and slept. And at midnight there was a cry made, Behold, the bridegroom cometh; go ye out to meet him. Then all those virgins arose, and trimmed their lamps. And the foolish said unto the wise, Give us of your oil; for our lamps are gone out. But the wise answered, saying, Not so; lest there be not enough for us and you: but go ye rather to them that sell, and buy for yourselves. And while they went to buy, the bridegroom came; and they that were ready went in with him to the marriage: and the door was shut. Afterward came also the other virgins, saying, Lord, Lord, open to us. But he answered and said, Verily I say unto you, I know you not.

The phrase "slumbering saints" is a contradiction in terms, as saints are not supposed to slumber. When saints begin to slumber, Satan rejoices. When a saint is in a sleeping stupor, such a fellow will end up serving Satan. God is looking for saints who are wide awake. The moment you are slumbering, your spiritual senses are insensitive.

The Bible has described modern-day believers as those who love slumber. The evil record concerning the five foolish virgins is that while they were expecting the bridegroom, they slumbered and slept with the others.

When they finally awakened, they trimmed their lamps and found out there was no more oil in it. They were not counted worthy to meet the bridegroom. They must have loved to sleep, otherwise they would have filled their lamps with oil prior to sleeping.

It is crystal clear that those who fail to meet the bridegroom will regret eternally.

There are times when slumber can subject a believer to slavery. A slave differs from a freeborn. Slavery cannot grant you the liberty that is accorded to sons and daughters of God. Therefore, you must not allow sleep nor slumber to make you a slave in the devil's camp.

Prayer Points:

1.   Spirit of slumber, die, in the name of Jesus.

2. Lord, give me oil in my lamp and keep me burning, in the name of Jesus.

3. I shall not sleep the sleep of death, in the name of Jesus.

4. Fire for apostolic revival, fall upon me, in the name of Jesus.

5. My inner man, receive fire, in the name of Jesus.

CHAPTER THIRTY - ONE

A CLOSED HAND CANNOT GIVE NOR RECEIVE

Proverbs 11:24,26

There is that scattereth, and yet increaseth; and there is that witholdeth more than is meet, but it tendeth to poverty. He that withholdeth corn, the people shall curse him: but blessing shall be upon the head of him that selleth it.

To receive, you must open your palms. You are a giver when you open your hands. Giving qualifies you to receive.

The economy of God's kingdom has a stipulated law: givers are receivers. If you are tight-fisted, and you refuse to give, you are automatically disqualified from receiving. The hand of the giver will always receive. Since it is true that the hand of the giver will always be above, givers will always remain blessed.

People with closed fists will always complain that there is not enough. If you want God to bless you, your hand must be opened. You must keep on giving until there is a memorial in heaven concerning your generosity. Whenever God is looking for hands into which His blessings can be deposited, He will always seek hands that are open.

Your hand will remain a fist as long as you are

giving out nothing. But if you have formed the godly habit of giving again and again, God will always convey His blessings to your open hands. Seek out for what you can give out to neighbours, colleagues, and family members today.

The more you give, the more heaven will replenish your pockets and your store house. Remember, givers never lack.

Prayer Points:

1. Spirit of giving, overshadow me, in Jesus' name.

2. Power to spend for the kingdom of God, fall on me, in the name of Jesus.

3. Poverty is not for me. I am for prosperity, success and blessing, in the name of Jesus.

4. Power to prosper, my life is available, enter, in the name of Jesus.

5. Oh Lord my father, make me a kingdom investor, in the name of Jesus.

CHAPTER THIRTY - TWO

TO BE IGNORED IS WORSE THAN TO BE CRITICISED

Proverb 29:15
The rod and reproof give wisdom: but a child left to himself bringeth his mother to shame.

C riticism can be very healthy, if only you can view it positively. It is better when you are openly criticised. Being ignored is worse than being criticised.

Open rebuke may be painful, but, it is better when people bare their minds and freely express their reservations concerning our shortcomings. It is better to allow people to air their view and let out their grievances than to keep mute and consequently ignore you.

When people no longer speak and they begin to avoid you, it shows that there is danger. When you are ignored, it reveals that you have passed the healthy stage of being criticised. It is better to allow people to criticise you and you are no longer popular than to allow them to hail you when in the inner recesses of their hearts, they loathe and keep you at arm's length.

Happy are you when you are criticised or castigated for known and unknown faults of yours. It is far better to bear criticism than to get to a stage when people have to ignore you to avoid any form of conflict.

Prayer Points:

1.   I bind and cast out every unteachable spirit, in the name of Jesus.

2.   Oh Lord, help me to take criticism in good faith, in the name of Jesus.

3.   My father, surround me with good people who will always point out my mistakes, in the name of Jesus.

4.   Oh Lord, deliver me from the lie that I tell myself, in the name of Jesus.

5.   Spirit of pride, die in my life, in Jesus' name.

CHAPTER THIRTY - THREE

EVIL MAY TRIUMPH
BUT WILL NOT
CONQUER

Job 20:5

Counsel in the heart of man is like deep water; but a man of understanding will draw it out.

The triumph of evil is often shortlived. Evil will never triumph over good. Those who are given to evil may cut corners and come up with achievements by making so-called smart moves.

But sooner or later, temporary triumph will fade and good will conquer evil. You cannot make use of evil methods and come up with victory or triumph that will last. A shortcut remains a wrong route that leads nowhere. Even when evil triumphs temporarily, such a triumph will fizzle out at the end of the day.

A lot of people in this generation have resorted to the use of Machiavellian methods. They believe that the end justifies the means. They are grossly unaware of the fact that only God can determine the real end. The Bible has clearly stated that the triumph of the wicked or the joy of the hypocrite will ever remain short lived. If you desire real victory, you must be ready to follow biblical standards.

Those who follow biblical principles will reap biblical results. There are people who contrive clever plots and embark on schemes that are satanic, simply because they are bent on getting to the top by stepping on others. Such methods will never work.

In the ordinance of God: Evil can never triumph over good. Good will always prevail. The mill of God grinds slowly, but surely. The final victory belongs to those who follow the way of God. Evil will never win the utmost prize.

Prayer Points:

1. My enemies shall not rejoice over me, in the name of Jesus.

2. Let God arise and let every enemy of my destiny scatter, in the name of Jesus.

3. Any dark power trying to attack me to get promotion, fall down and die, in the name of Jesus.

4. Oh God my father, arise and deliver me

from my strong enemies, in the name of Jesus.

5.   Father, let me come out victorious in life's battles, in Jesus' name.

CHAPTER THIRTY - FOUR

ANYWHERE THERE IS A RACE, THERE IS ALWAYS A PRICE

Proverbs 10:4

He becometh poor that dealeth with a slack hand: but the hand of the diligent maketh rich.

There is always a price to pay when you need a raise. Such a price can never be compromised. You pay a price before you are promoted and you must pay another price to keep the promotion. When you desire to be moved to the next level, you must be ready to make fresh sacrifices. As you rise higher in life, there will be fresh demands for higher consecration and commitment.

When you are favoured with promotion, you must not lose sight of the fact that there is a corresponding price to be paid to make the promotion work. Failure to pay the price will turn the promotion to mere shadow-boxing.

To reap the benefit of promotion or an uplift, you must pay a price that will bring honey out of the rock for you. You need preparation to give what is required for the next level. These include prayer, polishing your personal image, better management qualities and ability to face challenges that attend higher levels in life.

Pay the price: it is the only way you can move

forward in life.

Prayer Points:

1. I shall not fall by the wayside, in the name of Jesus.

2. Oh God, empower me to run my race to the end, in the name of Jesus.

3. The grace to pay the price for success, fall upon me now, in the name of Jesus.

4. Every spirit of procrastination, die, in the name of Jesus.

5. You spirit of laziness, die in my life, in the name of Jesus.

CHAPTER THIRTY FIVE

THE HIGHER YOU DESIRE TO RISE, THE HIGHER WILL BE THE PRICE

Philippians 3:14

I press toward the mark for the prize of the high calling of God in Christ Jesus.

Prices are in gradation. The higher you want to grow, the higher the price you must pay. You can only occupy an outstanding position when you have paid an outstanding price.

The price you will have to pay will always remain commensurate with the height you want to attain. Exceptional height requires exceptional price. If you are only prepared to pay a low price, you will find it difficult to get to your high places. What matters in life is the level of price you are prepared to pay. Even the sky cannot be your limit if you are ready to pay an extraordinary price.

Getting to the top is easy when you are ready to pay the price. Nobody will be able to determine the height you will attain, if you are prepared to pay the exceptional price for quality.

Prayer Points:

1. I receive inner fire, in the name of Jesus.

2. Power to run through a troop, fall on me now, in the name of Jesus.

3. When others are being cast down, I will say there is a lifting, in the name of Jesus.

4. The grace to go an extra mile with Jesus, I receive it, in Jesus' name.

5. I shall get to my destination with ease, in the name of Jesus.

CHAPTER THIRTY-SIX

ALL HEIGHTS ARE SUSTAINED BY CORRESPONDING DEPTHS

Luke 6:47-49

Whosoever cometh to me, and heareth my sayings, and doeth them, I will shew you to whom he is like: He is like a man which built an house, and digged deep, and laid the foundation on a rock: and when the flood arose, the stream beat vehemently upon that house, and could not shake it: for it was founded upon a rock. But he that heareth, and doeth not, is like a man that without a foundation built an house upon the earth; against which the stream did beat vehemently, and immediately it fell; and the ruin of that house was great.

I n the economy of God, the higher you go in life, the deeper the depth that is needed to sustain the height you attain.

The foundation of a great edifice must be strong enough to sustain the edifice. When your heart is not sustained by a commensurate depth, a sudden collapse is inevitable. The higher the heart, the deeper the depth that must be attached to it. When God gives you a higher calling, you must be wise to back it up with a depth that will sustain it.

When you suddenly find yourself at a great height in life or ministry and your depth is shallow, disaster is inevitable. Herein lies the reasons behind tragic crashes, divorces and failures. There is no shortcut to greatness.

Any sudden flight that is not backed up by adequate depth will give birth to tragedy. As you keep growing higher in life, you must not lose sight of the fact that you need a good depth to support the unusual height.

Prayer Points:

1. Take me deeper, oh Lord, in the name of Jesus.

2. Hunger and thirst for spiritual growth, come upon my life now, in the name of Jesus.

3. Power to be rooted in the word of God, come into my life, in the name of Jesus.

4. I shall not fall from grace to grass, in the name of Jesus.

5. Any power that wants me to fail in life and ministry, fall down and die, in the name of Jesus.

CHAPTER THIRTY-SEVEN

IF MOSES COULD NOT ESCAPE THE JUDGEMENT OF GOD, NO ONE CAN

Romans 2:11
For there is no respect of persons with God.

1 Peter 1:7
That the trial of your faith, being much more precious than of gold that perisheth, though it be tried with fire, might be found unto praise and honour and glory at the appearing of Jesus Christ:

It is tragic that a particular physical law has become applicable in the life of many people. The law: the higher you go, the cooler it becomes, is a dangerous law, as far as man is concerned. A lot of people assumed the fact that they occupy high positions in life will grant them immunity from the judgement of God.

Beloved, God has no favourite. Whether you are a Moses or a Paul the apostle, the law of God is applicable to you. No one is close enough to God to enjoy immunity, as far as God's standard of holiness is concerned.

If Moses, a man with whom God spoke face-to-face and mouth-to-mouth, could not escape God's judgement, nobody will be able to escape. If a man who is privileged to enjoy close fellowship with God did not escape His discipline, nobody will.

God does not play favourites. Be warned.

Prayer Points:

1. I shall not grieve the Holy Spirit, in the name of Jesus.

2. I will not become a misfired arrow in hands of my Maker, in Jesus' name.

3. Oh Lord, let me see my sins as the sword that pierce You by Your side, in the name of Jesus.

4. Oh God, let me see my sins as the nails that bind You to the cross, in the name of Jesus.

5. Oh God, come as power and expel rebellious lot from my heart, in the name of Jesus.

Dr. D. K. Olukoya

CHAPTER THIRTY-EIGHT

THERE IS A DIFFERENCE BETWEEN TRANSFORMATION AND MOTIVATION

Hebrews 12:27-28

And this word, Yet once more, signifieth the removing of those things that are shaken, as of things that are made, that those things which cannot be shaken may remain. Wherefore we receiving a kingdom which cannot be moved, let us have grace, whereby we may serve God acceptably with reverence and godly fear:

James 1:21

Wherefore lay apart all filthiness and superfluity of naughtiness, and receive with meekness the engrafted word, which is able to save your souls.

You can listen to motivational messages and not be transformed. Motivational messages are good. Most of the time they work only on the mind. Inspiration however is far deeper than motivation.

A lot of people who are motivated experience only momentary excitement. You can listen to motivational messages without experiencing inner transformation. But, it is better to be transformed and renewed than to be motivated.

When motivation wears off, the moment of excitement dies off. Within a short time, whatever is heard easily fizzles out.

It is better to listen to the undiluted word of God and experience total transformation, than to be motivated and lifted on the spur of the moment.

Our generation cannot go too far with motivational messages. What we need are messages that will revive and transform our lives and destinies.

Prayer Points:

1.   Oh Lord, establish as a holy person unto You, in the name of Jesus.

2.   Give me that old time religion, oh Lord, in the name of Jesus.

3.   Let the fire of revival begin to burn in my soul, in the name of Jesus.

4.   Spirit of the end time, loose your grip over my soul, in the name of Jesus.

5.   Oh God arise, envelop me in Your fire, in the name of Jesus.

CHAPTER THIRTY-NINE

THE SHEPHERD THAT SLEEPS NEVER SEES HEAVENLY VISITATIONS

Proverbs 6:9-11

How long wilt thou sleep, O sluggard? When wilt thou arise out of thy sleep? Yet a little sleep, a little slumber, a little folding of the hands to sleep: So shall thy poverty come as one that travelleth, and thy want as an armed man.

If you are addicted to sleep, forget about divine visitations. Your level of alertness will determine the type of messages you will receive from God.

When you get too busy during the day and fall into deep sleep in the night, you may be too numb to receive the touch of heaven. If you give all the hours of the night to sleep, you are likely to miss out on what the Spirit wants to say to you.

If you want to receive divine visitation, you must be ready to spend a great deal of time praying serious night prayers which will, most of the time, prepare you for exceptional divine visitation.

If the shepherds had been asleep, they would not have seen the Star of Jesus. Those who had conquered the 'battle of the bed' will always grow spiritually. The best battle to fight and conquer is the battle of the night. Warriors who convert the night to moments of aggressive prayers are exceptional overcomers.

You must be on regular night duty as far as prayer is concerned. During the day, the attention span of an average person is very short, but the hour of the night is an opportunity for elaborate prayers and fellowship.

If you can learn how to make use of the hour of the night, you will experience astronomical spiritual growth.

Remember, champions are made in the wee hours of the night.

Prayer Points:

1. My spiritual eyes shall not go dim, in the name of Jesus.

2. I receive the anointing to see heavenly vision, in Jesus' name.

3. Let the angels of God minister to my spiritual needs, in the name of Jesus.

4. I receive angelic visitation, in the name of Jesus.

5. Holy Ghost, incubate me for signs and wonders, in the name of Jesus.

CHAPTER FORTY

WE CANNOT GET ANCIENT RESULTS UNTIL WE REVISIT ANCIENT PRACTICES

Proverbs 22:28

Remove not the ancient landmark, which thy fathers have set.

There is a great gap between modernity and ancient Christian practices. Modern methods of preaching, evangelism and praise worship cannot give anyone the result of old-time Christianity.

The old-time religion may not be popular these days, but it is what gave our founding fathers the legacy they have handed over to us.

If you have read the Acts of the Apostles thoroughly, you will discover that the depth of their Christianity is absent today. If we forget the faith of our founding fathers, we might miss out on the exploits which they experienced.

We need to go back to the Bible and imbibe the type of primitive Christianity which is fast fading out today. To get ancient results, we need to go back to ancient Christian practices. More than anything, we need old-fashioned prayer meetings, fasting, evangelism and scriptural worship.

God has not changed. What we need do is go back to the divine blueprint as revealed in the Scriptures.

Prayer Points:

1. Let the faith of our fathers come alive in me, in the name of Jesus.

2. Pentecostal fire, turn my life around to the glory of God, in the name of Jesus.

3. Spirit of worldliness, loose your hold upon my life, in the name of Jesus.

4. Anything in my life that hates righteousness, come out and die, in the name of Jesus.

5. Create in me a new heart, oh Lord, in the name of Jesus.

CHAPTER FORTY-ONE

IT WAS THE PRIMITIVENESS OF PETER, JAMES AND JOHN THAT GAVE THEM THRONES IN HEAVEN

Acts 4:13
Now when they saw the boldness of Peter and John, and perceived that they were unlearned and ignorant men, they marvelled; and they took knowledge of them, that they had been with Jesus.

Acts 17:6
And when they found them not, they drew Jason and certain brethren unto the rulers of the city, crying, These that have turned the world upside down are come hither also;

We need to go back to primitive Christianity. One of the tragedies of modern day Christianity is that psychedelic methods and flashy styles have replaced what can be described as primitive Christianity.

Peter, James and John were not Bible school scholars. What distinguished them is that they learn raw lessons at the feet of Christ. Most of the time, they obeyed the voice of the Holy Spirit without holding any conference with flesh and blood. Of course, they did not get the revelation of Christ through flesh and blood. What made the disciples and the apostles to stand out was their primitivity. They did not modernise the work of God. What secured heavenly thrones for them is the fact that they forsook all and followed Jesus.

I wonder how many people are ready to stand for the truth and be sold out to God today. Would to God that we have primitive people like Peter, James and John among the rank-and-file of present-day preachers of the gospel! Oh that we might be accused as people who are turning the world upside-down like the apostles of old!

Prayer Points:

1. Oh God my father, make me a wonder to my generation, in the name of Jesus.

2. Lord, help me to be sold out for You, in the name of Jesus.

3. Father, help me to practise my Christianity like the apostles did, in the name of Jesus.

4. I will make it to the end, in Jesus' name.

5. Lord, let Your grace be sufficient for me, in the name of Jesus.

CHAPTER FORTY-TWO

IT IS WHAT YOU KNOW THAT WILL MAKE YOU KNOWN

Job 32:18

For I am full of matter, the spirit within me constraineth me.

There is no substitute for knowledge. The quality of your knowledge will determine how far you will go and who you will become in life. If your knowledge is shallow, you will become shallow. What you know is what will make you known.

The type of knowledge that you have is what will determine your level in life. The more knowledge you acquire, the greater the height you will attain. What you know will determine where you will be placed. If you are mistakenly assigned to an office that is beyond your personal knowledge, you will be demoted sooner or later.

Your level in life rises or falls on the level of your knowledge. What heaven has deposited in your life is exactly what will advertise you. Hence, if you are loaded with treasure and knowledge, the world will soon discover your extraordinary qualities.

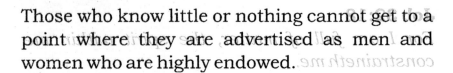

Those who know little or nothing cannot get to a point where they are advertised as men and women who are highly endowed.

Prayer Points:

1. Give me my personal Pentecost, oh Lord, in the name of Jesus.

2. Thou power of limitation, you are a liar, die, in the name of Jesus.

3. Evil progress, hear the word of the Lord, die, in the name of Jesus.

4. Birds of darkness assigned to trouble my star, die, in the name of Jesus.

5. My portion shall not be given to another in life, in the name of Jesus.

CHAPTER FORTY-THREE

IT TAKES GIANTS TO GIVE BIRTH TO GIANTS

1 Corinthian 11:1

Be ye followers of me, even as I also am of Christ.

You cannot give out what you do not possess. You cannot birth what cannot be found within you. You cannot produce what you do not possess. You cannot give a proof of what you have not experienced.

If you are a dwarf, your offsprings are likely to be dwarfs. If you are not a giant, you cannot be a giant's producer. If you are not exceptional, you cannot produce or mentor those who are exceptional. The quality you have is the quality you will produce.

You can only succeed in dazzling people for a short while. Soon, the stuff you are made of will be visible. If your profession is larger than life, your possession will reveal your true worth. To produce giants, you must have assumed the status of a giant.

Prayer Points:

1. Every power, holding tight to my instrument of advancement, die, in the name of Jesus.

2. Every enchantment assigned for my downfall, die, in the name of Jesus.

3. My father, arise and let the root of hardship in my life die now, in the name of Jesus.

4. Resources of heaven, arise by fire, and promote me, in the name of Jesus.

5. Oh God, my father, burst forth in my life by signs and wonders, in the name of Jesus.

CHAPTER FORTY-FOUR

IT TAKES A BIRD TO HAVE FEATHERS

Ezekiel 17:3

And say, Thus saith the Lord GOD; A great eagle with great wings, longwinged, full of feathers, which had divers colours, came unto Lebanon, and took the highest branch of the cedar.

Ezekiel 17:7

There was also another great eagle with great wings and many feathers: and, behold, this vine did bend her roots toward him, and shot forth her branches toward him, that he might water it by the furrows of her plantation.

B irds are known by their feathers. Your feathers will reveal your capacity to fly. If you are not a bird, the gravitational pull will bring you down each time you attempt a flight. If you are called a bird, but your wings and your feathers are clipped, you will lose the power of flight. If your feathers are weak, you will be incapacitated, and you will not be able to soar into the sky.

Do not call yourself a bird if you have no feathers.

Prayer Points:

1. I snatch all the keys to my success and multiple breakthroughs in the hands of my enemies, in the name of Jesus.

2. Oh God, dig me deep and fill me to overflowing with living waters, in the name of Jesus.

3. Resources of heaven, arise by fire, and promote me, in the name of Jesus.

4. Every Goliath boasting against my breakthroughs, die, in the name of Jesus.

5. Anointing attached to my name, scaring opportunies away from me, die, in the name of Jesus.

CHAPTER FORTY-FIVE

A TREE THAT IS NOT TALLER THAN YOU CANNOT SHADE YOU

Matthew 13:32

...Which indeed is the least of all seeds: but when it is grown, it is the greatest among herbs, and becometh a tree, so that the birds of the air come and lodge in the branches thereof.

You must locate a tree that is far taller than you, if you must come under a comfortable shade. Nobody can give you what he or she does not possess.

To receive higher anointing, you must locate someone who is more spiritually-endowed than you are. It takes a tree taller than you to give you enough shade. If you are taller than the tree, you will remain under the heat of the sun.

Beloved, you are responsible for the decision of coming under a tree that is taller than or a tree that is shorter than you. The level of shade you obtain will depend on the choice you make.

Prayer Points:

1. Oh Lord, lead me to the rock that is higher than I, in the name of Jesus.

2. Father, help me to locate my destiny helpers, locate me by fire, in the name of Jesus.

3. I shall not miss my destiny helpers, in the name of Jesus.

CHAPTER FORTY-SIX

LOVE GOD AND YOU WILL LOVE GOD'S PEOPLE WHEREVER YOU GO

Proverbs 10:12

Hatred stirreth up strifes: but love covereth all sins.

1 Peter 4:8

And above all things have fervent charity among yourselves: for charity shall cover the multitude of sins.

One major index of your love for God is your love of God's people. You cannot claim that you love God and be indifferent to His people.

When you truly love God, you will always love His people wherever you go. Love does not discriminate.

When the love of God is in your heart, you will love God's people everywhere, and you will be at home with them.

Prayer Points:

1. Spirit of love, envelop my life, in the name of Jesus.

2. Let the fruit of the spirit geminate in the

garden of my life, in the name of Jesus.

3. Teach me to love God's people, oh Lord, in the name of Jesus.

4. Every root of bitterness springing up in my heart, die now, in the name of Jesus.

5. Spirit of anger, die, in the name of Jesus.

CHAPTER FORTY-SEVEN

PERFECT PEACE COMES TO OUR HEARTS THROUGH OBEDIENCE

Job 36:11
If they obey and serve him, they shall spend their days in prosperity, and their years in pleasures.

Philippians 4:7
And the peace of God, which passeth all understanding, shall keep your hearts and minds through Christ Jesus.

There is no shortcut to perfect peace. The pathway of obedience is the fastest and the surest way to the land of peace. There is no peace for the disobedient: it is only absolute obedience that can induce absolute peace.

When you obey God in every area of your life, you will experience peace that passes all understanding. If you want to enjoy peace that the world cannot take away, you must be obedient to God even when it is not convenient. When you are obedient, the peace of God will be like shield and buckler in your heart. You will enjoy rest, assurance and absolute tranquility.

Prayer Points:

1. Let the peace of God, saturate my heart, in the name of Jesus.

2. Peace like a river, flow into my heart, in Jesus' name.

3. Lord, let me walk in the way of righteousness, in the name of Jesus.

4. I shall not engage in rebellion against God, in the name of Jesus.

5. Spirit of disobedience, die, in the name of Jesus.

CHAPTER FORTY-EIGHT

ALLOW CRITICISM TO SHAPE, BUT NOT CONTROL YOU

Romans 12:3

For I say, through the grace given unto me, to every man that is among you, not to think of himself more highly than he ought to think; but to think soberly, according as God hath dealt to every man the measure of faith.

Romans 14:4

Who art thou that judgest another man's servant? To his own master he standeth or falleth. Yea, he shall be holden up: for God is able to make him stand.

If you are criticised, you should endeavour to listen to what the critics are saying. If it is true, make amends, but if it is not true, disregard it.

You need criticism if you must grow and get better in life. A good measure of criticism is healthy. Criticism can make you better if it is properly handled. However, you must not allow criticism to affect you negatively.

Any criticism that leaves you discouraged, hopeless and despondent is unhealthy. Through criticism you can tighten certain loose ends in your life. Criticism can shape your

Olukoya

destiny positively. But when criticism begins to damage your inner motivation and weaken your morale, you can ignore such criticism. There is a time to listen to (constructive) criticism. There is also a time to ignore (destructive) ones.

Whatever will shift your focus and stifle your creativity is unhealthy. But you can embrace any criticism that helps you to rediscover yourself, increase your productivity, and build up your life.

Prayer Points:

1. I shall not be an old king that is resistant to advice, in the name of Jesus.

2. Lord, let me remain focus even in the face of criticism, in the name of Jesus.

3. I shall not be confused, I shall be calm, in the name of Jesus.

4. Agent of confusion assigned against me, die, in Jesus' name.

5. I renew my mind in the word of God, in the name of Jesus.

CHAPTER FORTY-NINE

HE WHO DOES NOT RECOGNISE THAT HE IS IN A RACE IS BOUND TO LOSE THE RACE

1 Corinthian 9:24-26

Know ye not that they which run in a race run all, but one receiveth the prize? So run, that ye may obtain. And every man that striveth for the mastery is temperate in all things. Now they do it to obtain a corruptible crown; but we an incorruptible. I therefore so run, not as uncertainly; so fight I, not as one that beateth the air:

You must be conscious of the fact that you are running a race. The moment you forget the fact that you are a key contestant in a race, you are bound to lose that race.

A major contestant cannot afford to be a spectator. A sportsman who has turned himself or herself to a spectator will lose the race.

You must be conscious of the fact that you cannot afford to be absent-minded in the race of life. You must be alert and run to win the coveted prize, which is the crown of righteousness that Christ has reserved for those who run, and win the race of life.

Prayer Points:

1. Lord, give the power not to fail in my spiritual walk with You, in the name of Jesus

2. Keep me as the apple of thy eye, oh Lord, and hide me under the shadow of Your wings, in the name of Jesus.

3. I will not end my journey halfway, in the name of Jesus.

CHAPTER FIFTY

FOR THINGS TO GET BETTER, YOU MUST GET BETTER; FOR THINGS TO CHANGE, YOU MUST CHANGE.

Joel 2:13

And rend your heart, and not your garments, and turn unto the LORD your God: for he is gracious and merciful, slow to anger, and of great kindness, and repenteth him of the evil.

You need to sit down and think deeply about these words. There was an Israel inside Jacob but the Jacob buried the Israel for 40 years.

A battle is required for you to bring out the Israel that is in you – an anointing is required for you to get to that place God had destined for you.

What happen depends on you. If you want a thing to get better, you must take an inward look. Change must begin with you. If you are not prepared to get better, there is no way things will get better. If you are not ready for a change, change cannot come.

Change must begin with you. You need to look inward and prepare for the type of change you have envisaged. Change cannot come when you remain your natural self. You must allow God to begin with you, then your change will naturally manifest.

Prayer Points:

1. Oh Lord, break and remould me to Your glory, in the name of Jesus.

2. Change my heart oh God, make it ever new, in the name of Jesus.

3. My father, do what You need to do to make me a better person, in the name of Jesus.

CONCLUSION

What you have read so far in this book can only be of benefit to you if you are ready to pray aggressively. Your life needs a radical change.

You cannot afford to remain the same. You must pray until you are totally transformed.

The onus of conforming to the image of Christ depends on you. The journey to the mountain of transformation must begin today. Pray until you experience far-reaching changes in your life.

Prayer Points

1. My Jacob, hear the word of the Lord, release my Israel, in the name of Jesus.

2. I fight from my Jacob to my Israel by the power in the blood of Jesus, in Jesus' name.

3. Every spirit of retrogression in my life, your time is up, die, in the name of Jesus.

CHRISTIAN PUBLICATIONS BY DR D K OLUKOYA
English Books
1. 100 Facts About Idolatry
2. 100 Weapons For Spiritual Warfare
3. 20 Marching Orders To Fulfill Your Destiny
4. 30 Things The Anointing Can Do For You
5. 10 Reasons, 10 Rules, and 10 Weapons
6. 30 Prophetic Arrows From Heaven
7. A-Z of Complete Deliverance
8. Abraham's Children in Bondage
9. Basic Prayer Patterns
10. Battle Cry Compendium (Vols 1,2,3& 4)
11. Battle Against Wasters
12. Be Prepared
13. Becoming Extraordinary Among The Ordinary
14. Bewitchment must die
15. Biblical Principles of Dream Interpretation
16. Born Great, But Tied Down
17. Born To Overcome
18. Breaking Bad Habits
19. Breakthrough Prayers For Business Professionals
20. Bringing Down The Power of God
21. Brokenness
22. Can God Trust You?
23. Can God?
24. Command The Morning
25. Connecting to The God of Breakthroughs
26. Consecration, Commitment & Loyalty
27. Contending For The Kingdom
28. Criminals In The House Of God
29. Charge Your Battery
30. Dancers At The Gate of Death
31. Dealing With The Evil Powers Of Your Father's House
32. Dealing With Tropical Demons
33. Dealing With Local Satanic Technology
34. Dealing With Witchcraft Barbers
35. Dealing With Unprofitable Roots
36. Dealing With Hidden Curses
37. Dealing With Destiny Vultures
38. Dealing With Satanic Exchange
39. Dealing With Destiny Thieves
40. Dealing With The Powers of The Night

41. Deep Secrets, Deep Deliverance
42. Deliverance Of The Head
43. Deliverance: God's Medicine Bottle
44. Deliverance From Spirit Husband And Spirit Wife
45. Deliverance From The Limiting Powers
46. Deliverance From Evil Foundation
47. Deliverance of The Brain
48. Deliverance Of The Conscience
49. Deliverance of The Tongue
50. Deliverance By Fire
51. Deliverance Through The Watches (Revelational Knowledge)
52. Deliverance Through The Watches (Sexual Perversion)
53. Deliverance Through The Watches (Dealing With Satanic Dreams)
54. Deliverance Through The Watches (Ministerial Upliftment)
55. Deliverance Through The Watches (Supernatural Conception)
56. Deliverance Through The Watches (Singles)
57. Deliverance Through The Watches (Wisdom)
58. Deliverance Through The Watches (Stubborn Situations)
59. Deliverance Through The Watches (Total Breakthroughs)
60. Deliverance Through The Watches (Business Breakthroughs)
61. Deliverance Through The Watches (Healing)
62. Deliverance From Triangular Powers
63. Destiny Clinic
64. Destroying Satanic Masks
65. Discovering God's Purpose
66. Disgracing Soul Hunters
67. Disgracing Water Spirits
68. Divine Re-positioninhg
69. Divine Yellow Card
70. Divine Prescription For Your Total Immunity
71. Divine Military Training
72. Divine Favour and Mercy
73. Dominion Prosperity
74. Drawers Of Power From The Heavenlies
75. Dreaming Divine Dreams
76. Evil Appetite
77. Evil Umbrella

230. Too Hot To Handle
231. Turnaround Breakthrough
232. The Deep Truth About Marriage
233. The Signpost of Unbrokenness
234. The Lost Secrets of The Church
235. Unprofitable Foundations
236. Victory Over Your Greatest Enemies
237. Victory Over Satanic Dreams
238. Victory Over Death
239. Victory Over The Storms of Life
240. Violent Prayers Against Stubborn Situations
241. Violence Against Negative Voices
242. War At The Edge Of Breakthroughs
243. Wasted At The Market Square of Life
244. Wasting The Wasters
245. Ways To Provoke Vengeance
246. Wealth Must Change Hands
247. What You Must Know About The House Fellowship
248. When God Fights for You
249. When the Battle is from Home
250. When You Need A Change
251. When The Deliverer Need Deliverance
252. When Things Get Hard
253. When You Are Knocked Down
254. When You Are Under Attack
255. When Your Destiny is Under Attack
256. When The Enemy Hides
257. When God Is Silent
258. Where Is Your Faith
259. While Men Slept
260. When One Door Closes, Another Door Opens
261. When The Wicked Is On Rampage
262. When Your Labour Needs Deliverance
263. Woman! Thou Art Loosed
264. Your Battle And Your Strategy
265. Your Foundation And Destiny
266. Your Mouth And Your Deliverance
267. Your Mouth and Your Warfare
268. Your Turn Around Breakthroughs

269. Your Uzziah Must Die

BOOKS FOR SINGLES
270. 50 Reasons Why People Marry Wrongly
271. 100 Stepping High Instructions For Singles (Volume 1)
272. 100 Stepping High Instructions For Singles (Volume 2)
273. 100 Reasons Why Sex Must Wait Until Marriage
274. 34 Laws of Courtship
275. 40 Marriages That Must Not Hold
276. Your Marriage And Your Ancestry
277. Choosing Your Life Partner
278. Breaking The Yoke of Marital Delay
279. Dominion Prayers For Singles
280. Principles of Magnetising Your Divine Spouse

Bilingual Books (English and French)
281. God of Daniel
282. God of Elijah
283. The Gate of Your Life
284. Self Made Problems
285. Fresh Fire
286. Encourage Yourself
287. Deliverance From Excessive Loads
288. Destructive Location
289. Detained by The Grave
290. Destructive Dreams
291. Deep Secrets of The Enemy
292. Deliverance From The Rod of The Wicked
293. Deliverance From Evil Altar
294. Destroying Destructive Prophesy
295. I Need A Miracle
296. Power To Bind, Loose and Spoil
297. How To Pray When Under Attack
298. My Life is Not For Sale
299. Who Are You?
300. Your Time of Visitation
301. Disgracing Evil Local Weapons
302. When The Spider is Wearing A Mask
303. Destroying Destructive Prophecy
304. Receiving The Oil of Favour
305. Dealing With The Stones of The Wicked

306. Dedications That Speak Against You
307. Spiritual Weapons
308. The Battle Against The Wasters
309. Power Against Unclean Spirit
310. The Battle Against the Wasters
311. Dedications That Speak Against You
312. Spiritual Weapons

Bilingual Books (English and Italian)
313. Deliverance of The Head
314. Command The Morning
315. How To Obtain Personal Deliverance

Spanish Publications
316. LLUVIA DE ORACIONES

Book in Chinesse
317. Prayer Rain

Swahili
318. Command The Morning

YORUBA PUBLICATIONS
319. Adura Abayori
320. Adura Ti Nis Oke Ndi
321. Ojo Aura
322. NigbatiOniseIranseItunisileNiloItusile
323. PakuteAhon
324. GbigbeOgun Ti AgbaraBuburu Ile Baba Re

FRENCH PUBLICATIONS
325. PLUIE DE PRIERE
326. ESPIRIT DE VAGABONDAGE
327. EN FINIR AVEC LES FORCES MALEFIQUES DE LA MAISON DE TON PERE
328. QUE I'ENVOUTEMENT PERISSE
329. FRAPPEZ I'ADVERSAIRE ET IL FUIRA

ANNUAL DAYS PRAYER AND FASTING PUBLICATIONS

Dr. D. K. Olukoya

THIS BOOK AND MORE ARE OBTAINABLE AT:

* MFM Bookshop Akeju
54, Akeju Street, Off Shipeolu Street, Onipanu, Lagos.
Tel: +234 (0) 8095423649

MFM Bookstall Prayer City
1st Floor, Modern Shopping Mall, MFM Prayer City
Km. 12, Lagos Ibadan Exp. Way, Ibafo, Ogun State.
Tel: +234 (0) 8095419968,+234 (0) 8095424185

* MFM International Bookshop
13, Olasimbo Street, Onike, Yaba.
(MFM Int'l HQ)
Tel: +234 (0) 8095419964

* The Battle Cry Christian Ministries
322, Herbert Macaulay Way, Sabo, Yaba, Lagos.

* All MFM Church branches nationwide and Christian bookstores.